It's Not Depression

Discover Core Emotions, Connect to Your Authentic and Focus on the Present

BY Elnora Anderson

Copyright

Table of contents

Introduction

Depression originates from a complex combination of social, psychological, and biological variables. People who have gone through unfavorable life circumstances (unemployment, bereavement, traumatic occurrences) are more susceptible to acquiring depression. Depression may, in turn, lead to increased stress and dysfunction and aggravate the afflicted person's living condition and the depression itself.

There are interrelationships between depression and physical health. For example, cardiovascular illness may lead to depression and vice versa.

Prevention initiatives have been demonstrated to lessen depression. Effective community initiatives to prevent depression include school-based activities to develop a pattern of good coping in children and adolescents. Interventions for parents of children with behavioral issues may decrease parental depressed feelings and enhance results for their children. Exercise courses for elderly individuals may also be useful in depression prevention.

Chapter one

Depression

Depression (major depressive disorder) is a frequent and significant medical ailment that adversely affects how you feel, the way you think, and how you behave. Fortunately, it is also curable. Depression creates feelings of despair and/or a lack of interest in activities you formerly liked. It may lead to several mental and physical difficulties and can limit your capacity to operate at work and at home.
Depression is a mental condition that creates a continuous sensation of melancholy and lack of interest.

Though depression and sorrow have certain traits, depression is distinct from grief felt after losing a loved one or sadness felt after a painful life experience. Depression frequently entails self-loathing or a loss of self-esteem but grieving normally does not.

In grief, joyful emotions and happy memories of the departed frequently accompany feelings of emotional suffering. In major depressive disorder, the emotions of melancholy are persistent.

People experience depression in various ways. It may interfere with your regular job, resulting in missed time and poorer production. It may also impact relationships and certain chronic health concerns.

Conditions that may develop worse owing to depression include:

- arthritis
- asthma
- cardiovascular disease
- cancer
- diabetes
- obesity

It's crucial to recognize that feeling melancholy at times is a natural aspect of life. Sad and sad occurrences happen to everyone. But if you're feeling depressed or hopeless daily, you might be dealing with depression.

Depression is considered a significant medical illness that may become worse without adequate treatment.

Depression symptoms

Major depression may induce several symptoms. Some influence your emotions and some affect your physical. Symptoms may also be chronic or come and go. Not everyone with depression will have the same symptoms. Symptoms may vary in intensity, how frequently they arise, and how long they stay.

If you encounter any of the following signs and symptoms you may be living with depression:

- feeling unhappy, nervous, or "empty"
- feeling dismal, useless, and pessimistic
- weeping a lot
- feeling disturbed, upset, or angry
- loss of interest in activities and interests you formerly loved
- low energy or weariness
- difficulties focusing, remembering, or making judgments
- moving or talking more slowly
- difficulty sleeping, early morning wakeup, oversleeping
- appetite or weight fluctuations
- persistent physical discomfort with no evident cause that does not go better with therapy (headaches, aches or pains, digestive issues, cramping) (headaches, aches or pains, digestive problems, cramps)

- thoughts of death, suicide, self-harm, or suicide attempts

The symptoms of depression might be experienced differently among men, females, teenagers, and children.

Males may encounter symptoms connected to their:

- mood, such as anger, aggressiveness, irritability, anxiousness, or restlessness
- emotional well-being, such as feeling empty, sad, or hopeless
- behavior, such as loss of interest, no longer finding pleasure in favorite activities, feeling tired easily, thoughts of suicide, drinking excessively, using drugs, or engaging in high-risk activities
- sexual interest, such as reduced sexual desire or lack of sexual performance
- cognitive abilities, such as inability to concentrate, difficulty completing

tasks, or delayed responses during conversations

- sleep patterns, such as insomnia, restless sleep, excessive drowsiness, or not sleeping through the night
- physical well-being, such as weariness, aches, headache, or digestive issues

Females may encounter symptoms connected to their:

-
- mood, such as irritability
- emotional well-being, such as feeling sad or empty, nervous, or hopeless
- behavior, such as lack of interest in activities, withdrawing from social interactions, or thoughts of suicide
- cognitive abilities, such as thinking or communicating more slowly
- sleep habits, such as difficulties sleeping through the night, awakening early, or sleeping too much
- physical well-being, such as lower energy, more weariness, changes in

appetite, weight fluctuations, aches, discomfort, headaches, or increased cramping

Children may develop symptoms connected to their:

- mood, such as impatience, anger, fast fluctuations in mood, or crying
- emotional well-being, such as feelings of ineptitude (e.g., "I can't do anything right") or despair, crying, or intense sadness
- behavior, such as getting into trouble at school or refusing to go to school, avoiding friends or siblings, thoughts of death or suicide, or self-harm
- cognitive abilities, such as difficulty concentrating, decline in school performance, or changes in grades
- sleep patterns, such as difficulty sleeping or sleeping too much

- physical well-being, such as loss of energy, digestive problems, changes in appetite, or weight loss or gain

Depression causes

There are various probable reasons for depression. They might vary from biological to situational.

Common reasons include:

- Brain chemistry: There may be a chemical imbalance in regions of the brain that govern mood, thinking, sleep, hunger, and behavior in those who have depression.

- Hormone levels: Changes in female hormones estrogen and progesterone over various periods such as during the menstrual cycle, postpartum period, perimenopause, or menopause may all boost a person's risk for depression.

- Family history: You're at a greater risk of getting depression if you have a family history of depression or another mood condition.

- Early childhood trauma: Some experiences alter the way your body responds to fear and stressful circumstances.

- Brain structure: There's a bigger risk for depression if the frontal lobe of your brain is less engaged. However, experts don't know whether this occurs before or after the development of depression symptoms.

- Medical conditions: Certain illnesses may put you at increased risk, such as chronic sickness, sleeplessness, chronic pain, Parkinson's disease, stroke, heart attack, and cancer.

- Substance usage: A history of drug or alcohol usage might impact your risk.

- Pain: People who endure emotional or chronic physical pain over long periods are substantially more prone to develop depression.

Risk factors for depression

Risk factors for depression might be physiological, medical, social, genetic, or situational. Common risk factors include:

- Sex: The prevalence of serious depression is twice as high in girls as in men.

- Genetics: You have an elevated risk of depression if you have a family history of it.

- Socioeconomic status: Socioeconomic status, especially financial troubles and perceived poor social position, might raise your risk of depression.

- Certain medicines: Certain medicines including various kinds of hormonal birth control, corticosteroids, and beta-blockers may be connected with an increased risk of depression.

- Vitamin D insufficiency: Studies have connected depressed symptoms to low levels of vitamin D.

- Gender identity: The risk of depression for transgender persons is approximately 4-fold that of cisgender people, according to 2018 research.

- Substance abuse: About 21 percent of those who have a drug use problem also suffer from depression.

- Medical diseases: Depression is related to other chronic medical problems. Those with heart disease are nearly twice as likely to have depression as persons who don't, while up to 1 in 4 people with cancer may also have depression.

Types of depression

Depression may be split into groups based on the degree of symptoms. Some individuals endure moderate and transient bouts, while others experience severe and continuing depressive episodes.

There are two primary types: major depressive disorder and persistent depressive disorder.

Major depressive disorder

Major depressive disorder (MDD) is the most severe type of depression. It's defined by persistent feelings of despair, hopelessness, and worthlessness that don't go away on their own.

To be diagnosed with clinical depression, you must have five or more of the following symptoms during 2 weeks:

- feeling depressed most of the day
- loss of interest in most regular activities
- significant weight loss or gain
- sleeping a lot or not being able to sleep
- slowed thinking or movement
- fatigue or low energy most days
- feelings of worthlessness or guilt
- loss of concentration or indecisiveness
- recurring thoughts of death or suicide

There are numerous subtypes of major depressive illness, which the American Psychiatric Association refers to as "specifiers."

These include:

- atypical characteristics
- apprehensive distress\smixed features
- peripartum beginning, during pregnancy, or immediately after delivering birth\sseasonal patterns
- melancholy characteristics
- psychotic characteristics
- catatonia

Persistent depressed disorder

Persistent depressive disorder (PDD) used to be termed dysthymia. It's a milder, but persistent, kind of depression.

For the diagnosis to be established, symptoms must continue for at least 2 years. PDD might impair your life more than serious depression since it lasts for a longer duration.

It's usual for persons with PDD to:

- lose interest in usual everyday activities
- feel hopeless
- lack productivity
- have poor self-esteem

Depression may be treated effectively, but it's crucial to stay in your treatment plan.

Living with depression may be challenging, but therapy can help improve your quality of life. Talk to your healthcare practitioner about available solutions.

Chapter two

Side consequences of depression

Depression Symptoms, Causes, and Effects
Depression is likely to hit many individuals to some degree throughout their lives. According to the Centers for Disease Control and Prevention, 9.1 percent of respondents reported current severe or moderate depression. If you or someone you love is sad, it may cause a dramatic loss of interest in living life to the fullest, and can, regrettably, push a person to try suicide if left untreated. Help is available; contact our hotline to discover how to stop the cycle of depression.

What Causes Depression?

Many probable reasons for depression exist. It might be hereditary, meaning the patient has a family history of depression. Personal trauma and causes of stress, such as a broken relationship or a lost job, may also induce depression. Social isolation as the consequence of a disagreement with family and friends may be a significant cause, and some drugs, such as high blood pressure medication, have depression mentioned as a potential side effect.

What Are the Signs of Depression?

If you observe that you or someone you know appears to be sluggish, socially disengaged, or has decreasing physical condition, depression may be present. There are various physical and emotional indicators to look for when assessing if a person has clinical depression, but you should always get an official diagnosis before making a decision.

Natural depression therapies.

These steps may help you feel better – beginning right now.

1. Get in a routine.

If you're sad, you need a routine, says Ian Cook, MD. He's a doctor and head of the Depression Research and Clinic Program at UCLA.

Depression may pull away the framework of your life. One day dissolves into the next. Setting a modest daily plan will help you get back on track.

2. Set objectives. When you're sad, you may feel like you can't achieve anything. That makes you feel worse about yourself. To

push back, make daily objectives for yourself.

"Start very little," Cook suggests. "Make your objective something that you can succeed at, like cleaning the dishes every other day.

3. Exercise. It briefly stimulates feel-good molecules called endorphins. It may also have long-term advantages for persons with depression. Regular exercise appears to stimulate the brain to remodel itself in favorable ways, Cook adds.

How much exercise do you need? You don’t need to run marathons to gain a benefit. Just walking a few times a week might help.

4. Eat healthily. No miracle diet solves depression. It's a good idea to monitor what you consume, however. If depression tends to make you overeat, being in control of your food will help you feel better.

Although nothing is conclusive, Cook says there's evidence that meals containing omega-3 fatty acids (such as salmon and tuna) and folic acid (such as spinach and avocado) might help reduce depression.

5. Get adequate sleep. Depression may make it hard to get enough shut-eye, and too little sleep can make depression worse.

What can you do? Start by making some modifications to your lifestyle. Go to bed and get up at the same time every day. Try not to nap. Take all the distractions out of your bedroom — no internet and no TV. In time, you may find your sleep improves.

6. Take on obligations.

When you're sad, you may desire to draw back from life and give up your duties at home and work. Don't. Staying active and having daily duties will help you maintain a lifestyle that can assist battle depression. They anchor you and give you a feeling of success.

If you're not up to full-time school or employment, that's OK. Think about part-time. If it sounds like too much, try voluntary work.

7. Challenge negative thinking. In your battle against depression, a lot of the effort is mental – altering how you think. When you're sad, you rush to the worst conceivable conclusions.

The next time you're feeling terrible about yourself, use logic as a natural depression treatment.

You might feel like no one likes you, but is there real evidence for that?

You might feel like the most worthless person on the planet, but is that likely?

It takes practice, but in time you can beat back those negative thoughts before they get out of control.

8. Check with your doctor before using supplements.

"There's promising evidence for certain supplements for depression," Cook says.

These include fish oil, folic acid, and SAMe.

But more research needs to be done before we'll know for sure.

Always check with your doctor before starting any supplement, especially if you're already taking medications.

9. Do something new.

When you're depressed, you're in a rut.

Push yourself to do something different.

Go to a museum.

Pick up a used book and read it on a park bench.

Volunteer at a soup kitchen.

Take a language class.

"When we challenge ourselves to do something different, there are chemical changes in the brain," Cook says.
"Trying something new alters the levels of [the brain chemical] dopamine, which is associated with pleasure, enjoyment, and learning."

10. Try to have fun.

If you're depressed, make time for things you enjoy.
What if nothing looks enjoyable anymore?
"That's simply a sign of depression," Cook adds.
You have to keep trying anyhow.

As weird as it may seem, you have to work at having fun.
Plan activities you used to love, even if they seem like a job.

Keep going to the movies.
Keep going out with pals for supper.

11. Avoid alcohol and other drugs.
Substance usage is widespread among those who suffer from depression.
You may be more prone to resort to alcohol, marijuana, or other substances to cope with the symptoms of your depression.
It's unknown whether drinking and taking drugs promotes depression.
But long-term drug use might affect the way your brain operates and aggravate or contribute to mental health issues.

When you're sad, you might lose the knack for enjoying life, Cook explains.
You have to relearn how to do it.
In time, enjoyable activities actually will seem fun again.

Is depression curable?

Having depression may be challenging.
It's easy to feel despondent and wonder whether you'll feel this way forever.
Wouldn't it be amazing if it could just... go away?
Sadly, it doesn't work that way—but that doesn't imply you'll always feel the way you do today.

Treatment vs. cure

When someone is healed from a disease, it implies it's gone permanently.
Some ailments can't be cured—like diabetes.
Once a person has diabetes, they'll have it for the rest of their lives.
But even a lifelong ailment like diabetes may be cured.
People who take their prescriptions consistently and make certain lifestyle

modifications may live long and healthy lives.
These drugs and lifestyle modifications are therapies for diabetes.

Depression is the same way.
There's no cure for depression, but there are dozens of effective treatments.
People may recover from depression and enjoy long and healthy lives.

Chapter three

what to do with your sorrows

LOSING A LOVED ONE

You're heartbroken.
Maybe furious.
And trying to make sense of it all.
Why did this have to happen?
Why now?
What would life be like without the person you lost?

It would be nice if there was a straightforward explanation that would cover all scenarios and answer all queries.
Unfortunately, we don't always understand why things happen to us that seem so foolish or cruel.

Grief is a normal emotion of losing someone or something significant to you.
You may experience a range of feelings, including despair or loneliness.
And you could feel it for a lot of different reasons.
Maybe a loved one died, a relationship ended, or you lost your job.
Other life upheavals, such as chronic disease or a transfer to a new house, may also contribute to sadness.

Everyone grieves differently.
But if you understand your feelings, take care of yourself, and seek assistance, you can recover.
The Bible refers to "the secret of iniquity" (2 Thessalonians 2:7 KJV), implying there is a mystery to some of the things we experience, even after a loved one passes away.

The death of a child, parent, or friend is tremendously traumatic.
God permits us to experience a mourning process so we can deal with the suffering.
He understands your agony, sadness, and wrath.

You ache tremendously, but be confident that God understands precisely how you feel.

What Are the Stages of Grief/sorrows

Your sentiments may happen in stages as you come to grips with your loss.
You can't control the process, but it's useful to recognize the causes of your sentiments.
All individuals experience loss differently.
Though it is no longer regarded as the optimal approach to thinking about loss,

you may have heard of the phases of grieving:

1. Denial: When you first hear of a loss, it's common to think, "This isn't happening."

You may feel stunned or numb.
This is a temporary approach to cope with the surge of intense emotion.
It's a defense mechanism.

2. Anger: As reality sets in, you're faced with the pain of your loss.

You may feel frustrated and helpless.
These feelings later turn into anger.
You might direct it toward other people, a higher power, or life in general.
To be angry with a loved one who died and left you alone is natural, too.

3. Bargaining: During this stage, you dwell on what you could've done to prevent the loss.

Common thoughts are "If only..." and "What if..."

You may also try to strike a deal with a higher power.

Depression: Sadness sets in as you begin to understand the loss and its effect on your life.

Signs of depression include crying, sleep issues, and a decreased appetite.

You may feel overwhelmed, regretful, and lonely.

Acceptance: In this final stage of grief, you accept the reality of your loss.

It can't be changed.

Although you still feel sad, you're able to start moving forward with your life.

Every person goes through these phases in their way.

You may go back and forth between them, or skip one or more stages altogether.
Reminders of your loss, like the anniversary of a death or a familiar song, can trigger the return of grief.

How Long Is Too Long to Mourn?

There's no "normal" amount of time to grieve.
Your grieving process depends on several things, like your personality, age, beliefs, and support network.
The type of loss is also a factor.
For example, chances are you'll grieve longer and harder over the sudden death of a loved one than, say, the end of a romantic relationship.

With time, the sadness eases.
You'll be able to feel happiness and joy along with grief.
You'll be able to return to your daily life.

Do I Need Professional Help?

In some cases, grief doesn't get better.
You may not be able to accept the loss.
Doctors call this "complicated grief."
Talk to your doctor if you have any of the following:

Trouble keeping up your typical schedule, such as going to work and cleaning the home

Feelings of depression\sThoughts that life isn't worth living, or of hurting oneself

Any inability to quit blaming oneself

A therapist may help you examine your feelings.
They can also teach you coping techniques and help you manage your sorrow.

If you're sad, a doctor may be able to prescribe drugs to help you feel better.

When you're in severe, emotional pain, it might be tempting to attempt to numb your emotions with drugs, alcohol, food, or even employment.
But be cautious.
These are momentary getaways that won't help you recover quicker or feel better in the long term.
They may lead to addiction, sadness, anxiety, or even an emotional collapse.

Instead, try these techniques to help you come to grips with your loss and begin to heal:

Give yourself time.
Accept your emotions and recognize that mourning is a journey.

Talk to others.
Spend time with friends and family.
Don't isolate yourself.

Take care of yourself.
Exercise frequently, eat appropriately, and get enough sleep to keep healthy and energetic.

Return to your interests.
Get back to the hobbies that offer you delight.

Conclusion

Depression might cause your mental health to deteriorate. And then when mental health degrades, it gets more and more tempting to overthink. It's like a massive downward spiral. the worse you feel. And the worse you feel, the harder it is to take suitable action since emotions may cloud your judgment.

Facts to know

Elnora Anderson is a researcher who aspires to affect her generation, especially in the lives of people through teaching, inspiring speeches, and training in life skills that will boost mental health.

The book "is a pertinent answer to this widespread problem. It is an essential resource for everyone who is down in one way or the other to be able to have decent mental health.

Elnora Anderson's other books include:

- Loving Emotionally immature parents
- Techniques to stop overthinking
- The hidden habit of a lazy genius
- Handling anger

www.ingramcontent.com/pod-product-compliance
Lightning Source LLC
LaVergne TN
LVHW052108160826
845678LV00015B/3424

* 9 7 9 8 3 5 2 8 1 9 0 6 7 *